I0438543

A PARADIGM
FOR OUR
SCHOOLS

LEWIS L. WHITMER

Order this book online at www.trafford.com
or email orders@trafford.com

Most Trafford titles are also available at major online book retailers.

© Copyright 2013 LEWIS L. WHITMER.
All rights reserved. No part of this publication may be reproduced, stored in a retrieval system, or transmitted, in any form or by any means, electronic, mechanical, photocopying, recording, or otherwise, without the written prior permission of the author.

Printed in the United States of America.

ISBN: 978-1-4669-9071-5 (sc)
ISBN: 978-1-4669-9073-9 (hc)
ISBN: 978-1-4669-9072-2 (e)

Library of Congress Control Number: 2013907603

Trafford rev. 04/23/2013

 www.trafford.com

North America & international
toll-free: 1 888 232 4444 (USA & Canada)
phone: 250 383 6864 ♦ fax: 812 355 4082

Contents

About the Author

Born in a small community and raised in Eastern Arizona, the author gained a great insight into the world of education. In his early life, there were good teachers and poor ones. At an early age, he decided to become an educator and try to make a difference in the educational world.

He gained an AA degree from the Eastern Arizona College, a BA at the Arizona State University, and an MEd at the University of Arizona. He has attended other colleges, attempting to gain a broad perspective on the educational scene. He has taught in different schools in different states and also taught adult education at the prisons in California. He has seen teachers who fail and who succeed and kept track of the progress of each.

Being a very successful teacher, he has gained the respect of teachers, administrators, parents, students, and many other people in the educational field. Problems have arisen when the various administrations have created unacceptable guidelines where educational prowess was ignored and where political correctness became king. This has only happened two times, and both times, he has made out OK with the other involved people: vis., the peers, the parents, the students, and the other administrators.

The author worked for the California State Prison System for about fifteen years. He taught classes of English as a Second Language, Adult Basic Education 1, 2, and 3, and GED preparation. He was a teacher for five years and then a supervisor of academic supervision for a number of years. He also acted for more than eighteen months as a supervisor of correctional education programs within the prison systems at Vacaville, at San Quentin, at the Ironwood State Prison, and at the Chuckawalla Valley State Prison. He had a total of eighteen years in the various prison systems of California, Arizona, and New Mexico.

The author would like to see everyone interested in their own education and the education of their children and to be strong in their own right—to help themselves, their peers, and their children to gain a perspective on education as well as to assist their children in gaining that same perspective and understanding of the necessity of learning for successful lives.

There is power in education as well as understanding and self-gratification.

The most important part of the prisons is to teach the inmates to be good citizens and to teach them to help others within the system and after release. There are too many men's lives being wasted because they wanted what others had and didn't want to work for it. It is very important that each of us look at the situation of our lives and consider if we are guilty of any infraction of the law before we condemn another.

Foreword

A PARADIGM FOR OUR SCHOOLS

Working within the schools, one will sometimes get caught up in the long-term way of teaching. We realize that education has been taught for many thousands of years. However, we also realize, with all our modern equipment, there could be better ways of reaching the students. It is very important that teachers love to teach and to see others learn. A teacher cannot get jealous if he/she discovers a very intelligent student; rather, that teacher should feel very blessed. It is essential we help *every* student if they are at the top of the ladder or on the bottom rung. We sometimes think that a child will never learn, and then someone came up with the words *late bloomers.* Other times, the child may have a temporary block to learning and will bloom even later.

We have created a paradigm for our schools—a way to think outside of the box that will give each child the same chance to learn as much as possible for that child. A *paradigm* is defined as an answer or a model, generally referring to presenting a different way of looking at a specific method of doing things, or a list of all the inflectional forms of a word taken as an illustrative example of the conjugation of declension to which it belongs. I will use the first definition for this purpose.

When we take things out of the box, we must look at the parameters it now covers and assure ourselves the important items remain. In the event we strip too much from the original, the exercise will be completely useless, and unless we take from the given program, those things that are counterproductive and our process will also become unnecessary and ludicrous.

Please read the entire book so the many things listed will make sense. If you agree with some of these things, then the process is working.

Chapter 1

SCENARIO FOR A PROGRESSIVE SCHOOL

"Children are always the only future the human race has; teach them well."

There is __more than one way__ things could be changed to make schools more effective. This is one way. It can happen in a local school district, in county schools, and in state schools, and even with federal interference. It can be used in a pilot program or however desired. It will not interfere with the lessons, but it will only make them more productive.

I do not claim to have all the answers; however, being raised in the fifties, I was taught if you attempt to destroy something, you'd better have a way or two to fix it. Following is one way a school can change and be changed for the betterment of education and maintain and gain the help and appreciation of the parents as well as the teachers, students, and society.

All the people who help to educate the children are preparing the children to run the world. The education they receive will determine what part they will play in running their points of leadership everywhere.

Each parent should make at least two all-day visits to the school where their children are attending in the first six grades for each child. We know the parents are interested in their children's progress and in the grades above the sixth grade; they can be a little more passive. It is necessary that parents show they are interested in what goes on in the schools even when their child will attend later in the upper grades, in middle school, and in high school. This will be especially true when they enter college and graduate school.

Anytime a person is given control over a group, regardless of the age, that person is responsible for what happens in that scene. Parents need to go into the classrooms of their children and see what is happening. This is for two reasons: (1) to assure the teacher is in charge and has sufficient plans for each day, and (2) to be enlightened as to the things that are being taught to their children. The parent is not there to interfere but to understand if they are inclined to offer help a day or two a month, however much they can. These visits need to be by schedule and with the approval of both the administration and the teacher. Teachers can prepare a special lesson or have the normal lesson. It would be better not to change procedure so the parent can get a good understanding of what is being taught in order to help the child with any homework.

These visits should be (1) in the first nine weeks of school, and (2) in the last nine weeks of school. The first nine would be to see the classroom their child is in this year, and the second will be to check out the classrooms where the child will be in next year. We will get back to this shortly.

These visits would be a win-win situation. The teachers will get to know the parents, and the parents will get to know the teachers. The parents will have ideas that might help in the education process, and the teacher would have a pool of helpers for big programs.

Basically, this program could be set up through the PTA or through the school secretary so there would be no duplication in the school and there would be a better chance of success. It would also allow the parent to see how their child reacts to certain types of lessons. The best part would be for the parent to see their children and understand the discipline necessary in the class.

After the parents have completed both visits, they could be invited to fill out a survey form with recommendations for their child to be in Mrs. White's class or wherever the next year. This would then actually make them novices in the education part of the school.

There is little possibility that *every set* of parents would be able to help in the reading, writing, or math that the children are learning. Some would not be able to do these things. Parents, this is a good chance for you. You can learn right along with your child. If necessary, arrangements could be made to help those parents that need help in a nonthreatening setting. In fact, in the seventh grade through high school, if a parent wants to learn what their children are learning, they could request night classes to help them catch up with what is going on in schools today. This request would have to be met with enthusiasm so the kids would see their parents learning as much as they are. This would be a positive happening so the kids would see their parents trying to learn. They might even help them. That's OK, but the whole community would be the winner.

Many parents dropped out prior to completing their education. The children would really be proud of their parents, and they would also want to work harder so they wouldn't have to do the same thing in their future.

Setting up the Leadership of the School

All teachers, principals, and superintendents must have the proper license to perform the duties they are hired to do.

Teachers

Let's go back, to the point where the parents will recommend a teacher for their children. Let's face facts: the parents will have a working knowledge of the teachers as much as the kids do. In the event a teacher does not get a certain number of recommendations, the teacher will be placed on probation and hopefully will be able to gain the necessary number the next year.

For the teachers who get that magic number, their next year is secure. If they get half again of that number, they will be given a full-time aid, and if they get twice that magic number, they will become a master teacher and help either a new teacher or one who is on probation. The parents will get better at the process, and some will become teacher's aides, and others will make good volunteers.

In order to succeed, we must have the teachers and the parents working together. Until that happens, we will have too many chiefs and not enough

Indians—or too many bosses and not enough education happening. ***Please think about this.***

New Teachers

New teachers would be chosen by a committee. This committee would be made up of two teachers, one principal, one parent from the PTA or a parent whose child may be in the class next term, a representative from the superintendent's office, and two children in the sixth grade or higher. They would also have to have a meeting with one another and whittle down the applications to six prospects prior to interviewing anyone. This committee would interview and recommend with a number value two applicants from the list. The names would be given to the school board and the superintendent for hiring. Tenure could be given to teachers who fill their class every year for four years, subject to their ability to maintain their efforts in teaching.

Principals

First of all, the principals would have a term limit and be chosen differently than now. There would be a committee chosen from two parents, two older students, two teachers, one other principal, and the superintendent or a representative from the superintendent's office. The process would be much the same; however, the superintendent would take the name to the school board for ratification. The term limit would be three years, but the principal could apply the second time but not a third time <u>at that school</u>. Principals could move three times to different schools within the district before being returned to the classroom, being given a position in the administration's office, or being a superintendent by the following process.

<u>Superintendents</u>

The selection of the superintendent would be more or less the same as the principal. The superintendent would have a five-year term limit with two extensions by the committee. The second and third applications would be all. After fifteen years, it would be necessary to go to a new area or back to a principal position or back into the classroom.

These are recommendations due to the fact that the administrators get the idea that they are the owners of the school. They will not allow anyone to question them. Their decision is final unless they are overridden by one who has more authority. The use of parents, teachers, principals, and students will allow these individuals to have a choice, and the positions would not be full of politics. The choices of these individuals would be by those represented. The PTA would choose the parents, the student body would choose the student representatives, the teachers would choose the teacher groups, and the principals would choose the principal groups. It would be necessary to have a representative from the school board present and voting for the new superintendent.

This then would place the whole education of the children in the hands of the community it serves. The choice would be accomplished via applications of interested parties. To rule out different applicants would be by polling the chosen representatives. Some might think it would be a long, drawn-out affair, and if the participants want it to be, it would be; however, after a few experiences in the process, it would be better. We may caution you that the choice of persons of each committee should, as much as possible, be independent from the other committees other than in the election of the groups. Cliques should only have one representative on one committee.

Using this process would allow the parents to really be involved with the school and have a part in its operation. After they have chosen a person, they will be more willing to support their choice, and the chosen one would know their own value in the process. In the event of a person needing to be replaced during the year, the superintendent could make that decision.

Each person chosen would have to go through the same evaluations as are presently accomplished; however, if a person has too many negative reports, the committee would be called up to hear and decide. They would either reinstate the person being evaluated or choose from a list of applicants. This, however, would be the choice of the committee, and the leadership would <u>have</u> to go along with it.

The person charged could be suspended, sanctioned, returned to duty, or could receive a recommendation for discharge. Reasons would have to be given for any of the above actions; the person charged would be able to defend himself and be present when the final decision is made.

This process is completely foreign to the present ways; all too often, people are discharged for no written reason, and those wanting to know what happened are given different answers. If the charges are serious and are a violation of the law, so be it, and the person should be charged in court, not on the opinion poll. Life goes on, and if a serious mistake is made, it should be made in the open and not under the table with gossip and innuendos.

These points should be thought out, used where comfortable, and not used unless there can be a complete democratic solution to it. I realize it takes the school of an area out of the hands of a small group and places it in the whole community and allows open reasoning as to the things that happened. Yes, there may be reputations damaged, but think of who is responsible for that damage. Who is the most important participant in the school? In my opinion, it is the students, and all things that are done must be done to help more students succeed. This method is not the only good method; however, my hope is that it will cause discussions, and perhaps changes can be made in our schools, and the schools can be the best in the world.

To gain and use the expertise of the parents, their love for their children, their abilities in helping their children, and their desire to work harder and learn more for the benefit of their children, we may have to offer a basic education to our parents. This will help the undereducated parents and, in turn, help the children of those parents understand the importance of education. Attitudes can be improved on every level of education. Industry will realize the potential of happier parents and workers with the understanding of their employees' children, making greater progress in learning, and this will improve their future employees.

IF YOU ARE NOT BUSY LIVING, IT ONLY GOES TO FOLLOW, YOU ARE BUSY DYING.

Chapter 2

EXPECTATIONS

Expectation levels are very important. If the teacher expects the child to perform at a certain level and the child thinks he/she can reach that level, the child should try. The teacher and the parents should support the child. If the child fails, they should be applauded for trying. They probably accomplished more than they would have without the expectation attempt.

When the student is in the fifth grade, it doesn't mean he is doing fifth-grade work. Students are passed on for many reasons: age, size, parent request, and many other unacceptable excuses. Instead of working with the student and bringing up their abilities, too often, he/she is allowed to slip by.

Students who have been beaten down all their scholastic life will not try to improve on their own. They have to be told they can learn, and many times, they have to be shown they can succeed. This responsibility falls directly on the teachers and the parents. We can recognize they have been told they have problems, but the extent of that problem cannot be realized until, each year, they make another attempt to learn. It doesn't take too much time, but the attempt needs to be made for the sake of the child.

Teachers may feel they don't have the time for that one child, but they do. Think of all the time you waste looking at the homework and grading it. Think of what the child thinks of him/herself to know they always fail. Give them a chance to fail or succeed at the level they are comfortable in. Make a contract, either written or verbal. Let the parents be a part of that contract, and enlist their assistance.

I would like to tell of an experience that happened to me. When I was in the sixth grade, my parents wanted to go to Phoenix for Christmas. They had some friends there who wanted us to visit. Upon arrival, the adults wanted to play minigolf, and they wanted us children to go to the movies. It was OK with us as we had never seen a movie in a theater before because in our hometown, there were not any.

The other family had three children: two boys and one girl. We also had two boys and one girl. They had a Ford Model A, with a rumble seat in the back where the trunks are today. Their three kids jumped in the back and left the front for my family. My sister sat in the middle next to the driver; my brother sat next to the door, and I had to sit on his lap. I didn't want to put my back on his face, so I turned and placed my back to the door.

When we got close to the bus stop, we were told to jump out when the car stopped and run for the bus. She said she didn't want to go all the way downtown. My brother got in a hurry and opened the door too soon. I fell out on the top of my head and lay on my back in the mud, with my face half submerged in the mud. They thought my neck was broken. It wasn't. The other kids went on to the movies, and I went to the hospital.

I was unconscious for two days, and when I woke up, I saw a lady sitting next to my bed. I asked her who she was; she told me she was my nurse.

Not understanding, I replied, "I'm hungry."

She said she could get me a bowl of soup. I had to resign myself to that, and she left.

As soon as she went out the door, another lady walked in. She came over to me, placed her hand on my forehead, then she glided her hand down my cheek. Finally, she bent over and kissed me in the middle of my forehead.

When the nurse returned, I took the soup and then asked her, "Who was that nice lady who came in when you left?"

Her eyes filled with tears, and she stated, "That was your mother." She left and came back with my father, my mother, my brother, and my sister, and she introduced them to me. Things were getting better all the time. I had a loss of memory.

I had to stay in the hospital for two weeks prior to going back to school. My teacher came up to me and asked if I had amnesia, and I nod my head yes. She said, "Good. Before, you wrote with your left hand. Now you will write with your right hand." Although my natural hand was left, she insisted I had to write with my right hand. Little did she understand that I had to do everything like before in order for my memory to return properly.

When I wrote with the right hand, my head would ache, and when I wrote with my left hand, she would hit me with a ruler on its sharp side. I refused to write, and she sat me in the back of the room. So it went like that for the remainder of the sixth grade.

When I got in the seventh grade, I was assigned to a teacher named Ms. Doolittle. She taught English and taught me how to write with the right hand. She also taught me how to read and write words and sentences and taught me the different uses of words: vis., nouns, verbs, etc. By the end of the eighth grade, I had caught up with my class in reading, writing, and sentence structure.

In the ninth grade, I was placed in a math class with Mrs. Park. She knew I had no math skills and taught me how to write numbers—how to add, subtract, multiply, and divide. I also learned fractions, decimals, algebra, geometry, trig, and calculus. I graduated number 12 out of seventy-two in the class.

These two teachers saved my academic life. I wasn't placed in special education. I wasn't forced to quit school after the eighth grade, and I really have done well for myself, but it would have been different if not for for those two teachers.

I am hoping that I can be as good a teacher as Ms. Doolittle and Mrs. Park were, and I hope the parents will be as supportive to each child as my parents were. Sometimes, children can't learn; sometimes, they are hyper and uncontrollable.

Many young people could learn if they were given the chance and if the teacher does not think them lazy but understands that they have a different problem. It would really be nice if the teachers could remember their utopian dreams they had at the age of their class members and in some way allow their class to live in that realm.

Our county, our schools, and our lives were begun with a religious guide, not some of the ne'er-do-well attitudes who want their ways to replace that which the United States of America has as its foundation.

They want to create laws that change morality, criminal activity, goodness, helpfulness, and many more aspects of the "American way of life." Every constitution of every state gives credence to the Almighty in one way or another. We need to get rid of what is called politically correct and help others to realize how to treat each other so we can be correct in this method. Actually, we are creating a more *prejudiced society* than we had before. Animosities are created by people who want to change the way other people live. If the way we live is offensive or hurts others, it needs to be changed, and those who did the poor treatment receive their own treatment so they can learn that all of us have rights and things that can't be changed to please a minority and hurt everyone else.

When changes are made, they must be worked out by the members of each side, and they must surely be solid. Most people in each side present their thoughts prior to activation or change of any kind. When our country makes changes, rules are made that will be broken on the backs of some individuals. It is too bad that compromise can't be created by two then four and up the ladder so all persons on each side can come on line without the sad consequences of things in our history.

A very great man once repeated a statement when he said "Love your neighbor as you love yourself."

In his day, as well as this day, this is still very good advice.

Judges have made poor choices, and most of the time, they will not humble themselves and change their findings. Here is a story where one judge did.

In a western state, there was a young man of sixteen years old who wanted a motorcycle. His father, a lawyer and well-to-do, informed his son that he would have to earn the money if he wanted one. The young man was sad then mad and returned to his father and stated something like this: "You are a successful lawyer and have a lot of money. I can't earn enough for a motorcycle for about two years." He then demanded he be given the motorcycle. The father remained strong in his answer.

The young man then took his father to the courts and sued him. At first, the judge didn't want to hear the case, but the boy was very persuasive, and the judge relented.

The father wasn't upset even though he had bad dealings with this judge before. He set up his defense, and the judge gave the son a lawyer to make things even.

After hearing both sides of the story, the judge took the case under advisement. Knowing what might come out of the hearing, the father prepared for the worst.

On the date of the next hearing, the judge found the case in favor of the son. The father was calm, walked up to the judge, and handed him an envelope. When the judge read it, he stated to the father, "You can't do this." The father responded, "You made a decision that would make it impossible for me to be a proper father. Unless you change your findings, my note stands."

Wanting to know what was in the note, the defense asked to join in to the sidebar. The judge responded to the defense, "It won't be necessary. With this evidence, I must reverse my decision." The defense wanted to know what that evidence was.

The judge stated, "I have been handed a paper of adoption. The father of the boy states that if I want to make rules of how to raise the boy, I should take full responsibility of him. I cannot break up a family and therefore reverse my decision."

The son went on to work for nineteen months and earned sufficient money to make a down payment. Therefore the father stated, "You have proven you really want and need the motorcycle, and since you have saved a substantial amount, I will give you an early birthday present for the cycle you want. You have to realize you will have to pay for the gas and the other upkeep for yourself." The son thanked his father and learned a great lesson.

When a child, regardless of the age, gets the impression that he can have anything he wants just by asking, that child must learn that he has to be responsible and earn that item. Some parents had little when they were growing up, and now they have a lot. They seem to not want their children to want for anything. The idea is good, but the child has to know these desires need to be fulfilled with some effort on their part.

My parents would mention the other kids were spoiled, and then I would think of spoiled food, rotten eggs, etc., and in my growing up, if I wanted special things, I had to participate in securing that item. Sadly, some children are taught, "If you want something, take it, but don't get caught." The young people try that, and the older kids help them learn how not to be caught.

It is a sad case to have the parents misinformed, and with respect to that misinformation, it is a case of abuse in the worst kind. Older kids take things they want, and the smaller children learn from the older ones. It will never end until the parents, the teachers, and the other adults take charge and make it not happen.

Teachers need to know their children. This can best happen when they get to know the parents of these children. Enlist the parents to help teach manners and other social skills that will allow that child to be better accepted in society. All children must learn to share what they have by their own volition and not by force. Often, when a child cannot have what other children have, they will try to get something in any way they can. Stealing, robbing, bullying, and other methods of coercion will teach that child to be dishonest all his/her life. That child has a poor beginning.

In the event there is a special need for a child, the parents, the teachers, and the support groups should get together and help the child to be better adapted in the school environment. The special need should be addressed, and a plan of action should be developed with all the parties participating. In many cases when the program is somewhat developed, if possible, invite the child to be present, and allow his ideas to be used as is possible. Remember, if the child will hear what is necessary and what needs to be done on his part, it will help him to buy into the program.

Don't set unrealistic goals or expectations, which would be a plan for failure. Rather, allow the child a chance to succeed, even if that success is small. Don't overwhelm him, and when he is home, suggest he does his work that is sent home with him. Allow him ownership in the success and the failure. He will appreciate the success if he knows how he got there.

Parent-teacher meetings should be scheduled beginning with kindergarten as well as ending after the sixth grade, unless the child needs the extra help. Teach them there is no shame for being helped to learn; the only shame is when the child will not try, or when the parent or the teacher rejects all attempts.

As mentioned previously, there are some things that do not belong in the school; they are not in its curriculum. There are better places for these things to be taught. I would like to list a few and, in some cases, with special circumstances that these things can be referred to. Reason with yourself if these things belong in public education.

__Sex Education, whims of special interest groups, women's liberation, sexual orientation, religious problems, and many other types of things that keep the child from learning those important parts of getting ready for a working situation.__

The courts have created laws and want these laws enforced. This is showing their lack of understanding what their jobs should be. Basically, they are to adjudicate the laws that the Congress and the President have made. Enforcement is to be in the hands of the local, the county, the state, and the federal officials. The jurists may have to evaluate the laws made by the proper individuals to assure they are following the Constitution, *NOTHING MORE, NOTHING LESS.*

Working with students, parents, teachers, and administration will give the student and the parents ownership and responsibilities of the education of the children to their adulthood.

The greatest honor a teacher can receive is to have the emulation of the child desiring to be a teacher and accomplishing it. It is gratifying to see our ex-students become teachers. It is better than to have them hate school and to teach their children to feel the same way. Knowledge is power, and proper use of it is a blessing to all the receivers.

After a child begins to think about his or her future, the parents, the teachers, and the other interested parties should help them as much as they can for the child to gain knowledge about that field of labor. It is much better not to argue or discourage but rather to help them find out the perimeters they will have and the preparation necessary and desirable, with the knowledge that anything worth doing is worth doing well. Your expectations should challenge the child and not frustrate them. There is a fine line, and you as an interested party must find that line and allow the child to find it as well.

Teachers and parents should discuss the child's future and assist each other as much as possible. Come to an understanding that the child's choice is more important than anyone else's. In the event the child wants to get into criminal life, take them to the law enforcement people to allow them to show them the good parts and the bad parts. Losing your temper and arguing will only solidify the child's choice. There are many things you may not want your child to try; as an adult with responsibilities toward the child's future, you may have to do some research on the matter.

If there is a problem between the teacher and the parents, try to solve the problem between yourselves first. Get a mediator next time, and if there is still division, have your child removed from the room. It is important that the child knows why there was a problem and that reasoning should come from both the teacher and the parents. Sometimes, the problem will be misunderstanding or perhaps a _**story**_ created for sympathy from one party or another. Think on these things, and be sure your choice is right.

Respect and learning go hand in hand. If the child is respected, he will respect. Authority needs to respect the rights of the child in order for the child to respect that authority. It is a two-way street, and respect cannot be required, mandated, nor insisted upon. It has to be earned. If both parties have respect, it is good.

Courts are a place where respect is demanded without even a whisper of returned respect. The tone of the voice, the words chosen, and many other things exemplify how one feels about another.

Don't be plastic; don't fake agreement if you don't agree. Conversely, don't fight over a point; that's what lawyers are for, and the others don't worry if the statements are stated without any emotions. At school, keeping order is paramount and necessary. A person who breaks the law should be turned over to the proper authorities. If the infraction is against the school rules, it is necessary to keep the problem in-house. Schools are responsible for school problems. Street problems belong in the streets. Lawbreakers need to be punished by those who created the laws.

This type of program will allow the children to gain self-esteem; it will allow the teachers to get more involved with those children who are above or below the level of the other children. For the one who says it won't work, it is suggested he/she opens his/her mind and try it. I did and succeeded.

When a teacher respects and therefore is respected, the child will have a better chance of gaining a good education. If the child brings a problem home, it is important for the parent to check it out. We cannot take everything said to be accurate. For the child, it may be true; however, we need to look at it with open hearts and minds. If you know something did happen, check it out, and gain your own perspective.

The following is one scenario that would involve a lot of changes in the various school districts in our country. Each event is viable in it and will function without the others; using all of them will help to work on many of the frailties of our public school systems. It is not desirable to have home schools or even private schools without the laws that the public schools have to work with.

Be honest with yourself, and study chapter 9 very closely before deciding the worth of it. I will state that it is not the only way to go, but it is one way that, in my years of teaching and administration, I have placed some of these methods within and wished for the others into the teaching year without the notice of the others and their realizing it was different.

Chapter 3

GENERAL EDUCATION PROBLEMS OF TODAY

Problems developed in the schools, not so much because of the teachers, but in spite of the efforts of the education departments. Parents and society, as a rule, wanted to abrogate their responsibilities for their children. They began to expect the teachers to be parents without any authority to discipline the children.

BIG PROBLEM

School dropouts are a very big problem. When we begin wondering why we have so many dropout children, we can start looking in the so-called inner city. There are many places to identify, many people who have dropped the ball. We can list parents, peers, older children, the child, and lastly, the schools. In actuality, we can also blame law enforcement and the judiciary. Let's give only one reason for each group listed above, and we are sure you can find others.

Parents

I can remember, while raising my children, there were ads stating on the TV and the radio, "It's ten p.m. Do you know where your children are?" Seemingly, in this day and time, the children are rebellious, or the parents don't care. Kids get involved with other kids, and many of them have already quit school, and your children feel that these things are OK. They can work in gangs, sell drugs, and exploit others in order to have money. The thing wrong here is that the parents don't ask where they got the money. This could be because of fear that the child would tell the parents. Some (hopefully a minority) parents are glad they are not asked for money due to their not having any. There are many reasons for this, a few not too bad.

Peers and Gangs

When the children get hooked up with their peers, they at first are the slaves of the gang. After they have proven themselves, they are regular members and recruit others to be part of the gang.

Older Children

These older children are predators and want others to be as miserable as they are. They realize the younger ones can commit a crime and not have to pay a bad price for it. Besides, this places that child in a gladiator school, so to speak. They learn more in the lockup than they could ever learn on the streets. The police are actually doing these older children a favor by helping to train the new kids to work for the gang.

The Child

When the child sees their friends getting short sentences, they realize it might be fun to experience it.

The Schools

When a child misbehaves at school, the schools are bound as to their reaction. They can send them home, but they never get there or leave soon after arrival. They can suspend them; this gives them cause to not want to return to school. They can punish them, making them stay after school and fulfill certain jobs within the school. Really, they can't do much to help the child. They can have parent-teacher conferences, but mainly, these children will not listen to the parents or the teachers.

Law Enforcement

Those of the law enforcement are required by law to treat the child with kid gloves. One time in my life, I asked the local sheriff to place my son in a cell for an hour or two for stealing from a store. He did, and it was successful for a time and did make my son think about what he was doing. I do not advocate placing the child in a cell with other felons but next door would be OK. They have to know the cost of committing crimes. The police should treat them like the other prisoners—place them in a holding cell for a period of time before their parents can see them.

Judiciary

The people in the courts think they are a gift to society. Many times, they create laws by their actions. This is wrong. Below are some examples I received from the Internet, and it can help more than my rhetoric.

School 1976 vs. 2006

From an e-mail, I received the following:

Scenario 1: Jack goes quail hunting before school and pulls into a school parking lot with his shotgun in the gun rack.

1976—The vice principal comes over, looks at Jack's shotgun, goes to his car, and gets his shotgun to show Jack.

2006—The school goes into lockdown. The FBI is called. Jack is hauled off to jail and never sees his truck or his gun again. Counselors call in for the traumatized students and teachers.

<u>Scenario 2:</u> *Mark and Johnny get into a fistfight after school.*

1976—A crowd gathers. Johnny wins. Johnny and Mark shake hands and end up best friends. Nobody goes to jail, nobody is arrested, and nobody is expelled.

2006—The police are called. The SWAT team arrives, arrests Johnny and Mark, and charges them with assault. Both are expelled, even though Mark started it.

<u>Scenario 3</u>: Jeffrey won't be still in class and disrupts other students.

1976—Jeffrey is sent to the office and given a good paddling by the principal. He returns to class, sits still, and does not disrupt the class again.

2006—Jeffrey is given huge doses of Ritalin and becomes a zombie. He is tested for ADD. The school gets extra money from the state because Jeffrey has a disability.

Scenario 4: Billy breaks a window in his neighbor's car, and his dad gives him a whipping with his belt.

1976—Billy is more careful next time. He grows up normal, goes to college, and becomes a successful businessman.

2006—Billy's dad is arrested for child abuse. Billy is removed to foster care and joins a gang. The state psychologist tells that Billy's sister remembers being abused herself, and their dad goes to prison. Billy's mom has an affair with the psychologist.

Scenario 5: Mark gets a headache and takes some aspirin to school.

1976—Mark shares the aspirin with the principal out on the smoking dock.

2006—The police are called. Mark is expelled from school for drug violations. His car is searched for drugs and weapons.

Scenario 6: Pedro fails high school English.

1976—Pedro goes to summer school, passes English, and goes to college.

2006—Pedro's cause is taken up by the state. Newspaper articles appear nationally, explaining that teaching English as a requirement for graduation is racist. ACLU files a class action lawsuit against the state school system and Pedro's English teacher. English is banned from the core

curriculum. Pedro is given a diploma anyway but ends up mowing lawns for a living because he cannot speak English.

<u>Scenario 7</u>: **Johnny takes apart leftover firecrackers from the Fourth of July, puts them in a model airplane paint bottle, and blows up a red ant bed.**

1976—The ants die.

2006—BATF, Homeland Security, and the FBI are called. Johnny is charged with domestic terrorism. The FBI investigates. His parents and his siblings are removed from their home. Their computers are confiscated. Johnny's dad goes on a terror watch list and is never allowed to fly again.

<u>Scenario 8</u>: **Johnny falls while running during recess and scrapes his knee. He is found crying by his teacher Mary. Mary hugs him to comfort him.**

1976—In a short time, Johnny feels better and goes on playing.

2006—Mary is accused of being a sexual predator and loses her job. She faces three years in state prison. Johnny undergoes five years of therapy.

Each of these scenarios has happened or will happen. Teachers are not able to help care for their students in any way.

Those who either hate school or go to lengths to degrade teachers have seemingly won some battles.

When education is less effective, kids start dropping out. When the schools teach unacceptable material, parents go to either home school or to private schools, unless the schools begin to communicate with the parents and the community about the curriculum and teach morals of some sort. Unless the parents have something to say in what is taught and some say as to who does the teaching, the productivity of the schools is at risk. When a person is elected to a position that has any control over the schools or if they think they should have such control, they will continue to propagate the things that eventually will negate any education.

In the rural community as well as in the inner city, schools are teaching things that relate elsewhere. Pictures and movies do not equate to actually being present at the site. When the teachers perhaps have not been to the places they are teaching about, how can they do an adequate job and help the children to really understand the manners and morals of the people? Now the teachers want to introduce the children to all things if or not they understand. They teach from the books and not from their hearts and minds. The leadership seems to want the teachers and the children to learn robotically, so they introduce the different aspects of the subject that were not taught until high school and even college previously, not looking for comprehension nor understanding but only to be on a certain page at a certain time.

History and geography are being forced down the child's throat without any understanding as to the actual position of the area or events. Previously, children were taught the things they understood and the places they heard about in stories. Now with the Internet, those in power seem to think all children have access to a computer and know a lot more than they actually do. Not everyone has access to a computer, and in fact, some parents cannot access the material from the computer.

It is true that each child needs to learn about the other parts of the world; we cannot expect them to understand the differences without being there and seeing the difference for themselves. The education process must allow the student to be a child or a young adult and not require them to give it up. It must not confuse the student. Students need to think for themselves and experience things they will have to make decisions about later. These things need to be told to the parents prior to the children and allow the child to be excused from them.

Foul language is supposedly not allowed in the schools, but when the teachers use these words, the child learns how they can also use the same word.

There are IQ tests that were developed many years ago for a completely different society. Of course, the children will not have sufficient scores to "be intelligent." Precollege tests are given to the seniors or the juniors, and if they get a certain score, they are OK for college; below that score, they need to attend a vocational college.

Teachers need to have the students pass certain information, so they teach the test rather than the material. The child has been introduced to the material but still do not understand it. With the No Child Left Behind program, the same thing is happening, but in the next year, the child will have to learn it all over again. This is where they **all** are being left behind.

WHEN WE UNDERSTAND THAT EVERYONE WANTS TO BE A TEACHER IN THE PUBLIC SCHOOLS, WE ALSO MAY UNDERSTAND WHAT PROBLEMS WE FACE. TEACHERS AND ADMINISTRATORS SHOULD RETURN TO THOSE THINGS THAT WILL AFFECT THE CHILD'S ABILITY TO MAKE A LIVING. LACK OF CONTROL IN THE SCHOOLS WILL LEAD TO THE PARENTS AND THE CHILDREN SETTING THE CURRICULUM.

PARENTS MUST BE MORE INVOLVED IN THEIR CHILDREN'S EDUCATION. SCHOOLS DO WHAT THEY CAN, BUT THE PARENTS

DON'T SUPPORT THEIR SCHOOLS, AND THE SCHOOLS DON'T SUPPORT THE PARENTS.

I found this poem and think it fits the situation well.

UNITY

I dreamed in a studio, and watched two sculptures
there,
The clay they used was a young child's mind, and
they fashioned it with care.
One was a teacher and the tools she used, were
books and music and art
One was a parent with a guiding hand and a gentle
loving heart.
And then at last when their work was done, they
were proud of what they had wrought
For the things they had molded into the child, could
never be sold or bought.
And each agreed she would have failed, if she had
worked alone,
For behind the parent stood the school, and behind
the teacher stood the home.

(UNK)

Chapter 4

BRIEF HISTORY OF EDUCATION

A brief discussion of the history of education will show that our education process has always been fluid. You will not find two decades with the same overall educational process. Teachers who teach all their lives will either have to keep up or fall by the wayside. In some ways, this is good, but in other ways, it is divesting to those teachers—to think that the process is ever changing and that those things that have been working so long are now not acceptable.

PARENTS' RESPONSIBILITIES

It is necessary that the education of the children, our children, need to have complete family cooperation. Children learn from their parents by watching and mimicking them. This has been the case since there have been children. At the very first, children did what their parents did. Parents were good teachers because they loved their children and mostly were proud of them. In that time, parents received their education in the same way, they were taught mostly by their parents.

Communication in that day was created by those moving around and wanting to leave information for others. Cavemen drew on walls. This marked their territory and told of the things that had aspired and perhaps told of their abilities. There was no thought of letters or symbols at first; however, these things finally came into being.

They created letters from pictures, and then descriptive words were needed to clarify the things they wanted to say. With these developments, communications were born and evolved in some areas, but in other areas, it took more time.

EDUCATION AND COMMUNICATION BECOMES POWERFUL

It soon became apparent that knowledge was power. It seemed that those who could read and write information and carry that information to others were becoming organized and showed a new intelligence. With this came the ability to gain control over others.

Religion and other beliefs were expressed and were passed on. Soon, songs were written along with other literature, allowing art to progress from the walls of the caves to the canvases or whatever they wanted to draw upon. With this aspect, education and any form of communication became organizers to the city states and the other forms of government. Religion began formal schools to teach their doctrine; others used this form of communication to teach leaders and other political entities to forward their own agendas.

Parents wanted their children to learn and use their education to have better places in the world. The parents wanted their children to know about the life they were living as well, so they continued to teach them things at home.

THE SO-CALLED DARK AGES

During the time of the Dark Ages, education took a backseat in life. This was the time of control by the strong and the wealthy and for the church leaders to gain the leadership roles and control of literally the whole earth. During this time, political aspirations became the key to growth. It seemed that LOVE had left the world.

At times, if a person attempted to teach openly, he was driven away or killed. Those that ran away started other types of communities and worlds. Education literally went underground. Near the end of the Dark Ages, books were the key to the Reformation. This was because the earlier points of the lives, the education, the families, and the organized communities began to question those who had taken control.

There were people who began again to strengthen education and to help others to learn to read and write but most importantly to think and use their ideas. We have Guttenberg, Luther, and other reformers as well as political leaders to help in this education.

Soon, education became important to everyone, and with knowledge came progress. Schools began again, mostly by the churches, the parents, and in some areas the community leaders. The world began to have inventions that were not just for war or for the conquerors. Educated people started questioning the divine right of the kings.

Looking at the whole picture, there were events all over the world, and people all over the world began to wake up to reality. I guess the only places that were not waking up were on the islands both Atlantic and Pacific. It is too bad they didn't gain the perspective of the other parts of the earth.

EARLY SETTLING OF THE AMERICAS

Everywhere that people settled where there were children, educational ideas woke up. Settlers came to the Americas from Spain, Portugal, France, England, Russia, and the Orient. They came for many reasons and were able to use their trades in the manner they desired. Each nation made settlements and began to rule and reign over the people like they had in Europe and Asia. It didn't work. These new settlers knew this was a new land, and they joined together and broke from their mother country. The sad thing was, they modified the methods of teaching and thought to make it new and exciting. This was like the oiler in a train, wanting to be the engineer and driving the train without having the proper training by someone who knew what he was doing.

New England's puritan emphasis upon the value of schooling brought educational leadership to this section. In 1647, Massachusetts required every town of fifty or more families to maintain a public elementary school, although many communities did not obey the law. By 1689, all of New England except Rhode Island had followed this example, with varying results. In the Middle Colonies, education was limited by the fact that it was regarded as a church rather than a public function. In the south, private tutors were hired by one or more families jointly where they could afford to do so, and public schools were not provided.

The Latin grammar schools of New England were about the only secondary schools in all the colonies. Of the nine colleges founded in the colonies before the Revolution, all were connected with religious groups with the exception of Harvard (1636), William and Mary (1693), and Yale (1701) that were three of the colleges that were started as training schools for religious purposes and teachers of common knowledge.*

Horace Mann began schools to train teachers, and other like schools began to pop up 1826-1836.

In other areas, schools were founded in the homes; next, in the churches and in the local municipal buildings. It was realized that some of the people did not want the children educated, and the school methods became manageable when run by the various municipalities. In the low-population areas where it could not happen, schools remained in the home. New buildings were constructed, and schools began to be manageable. The states took charge and eventually tried to have each school teach the same way.

---

* BARROW'S United States History: To 1877 pgs 50, 211.

Wars and other interruptions caused a slowdown for the schools, allowing others to catch up. They wanted all students to be the same. A little analogy here: if everyone was alike, and individuality ceased, all people would want the same thing. Marriage, family, and these other identifiers of our country would disappear; there would be no progress. We need to teach our children to be what they are, not what someone thinks they should be. When the schools realized that everyone was going in different directions, they looked for another solution. They still didn't get the big picture.

After the war that would end all wars—the First World War—recovery for the schools was slow, and by the time of the next war, education was placed on the back burner.

When the Second World War started, the country needed more teachers as most of the teachers were men. To fill the void, women began to be teachers. Their attempts were great. As one of my teachers put it, generally, the women are closer to the kids. They began to see progress.

This didn't work well, so school districts were formed. This was so the education would be related to the jobs, etc. in the area. The schools were maintained, and basically, the parents and the governments set up the schools and the curriculum.

The Constitution was complete, and the forefathers realized the best school leaders would be the states. They set it up that way, but eventually, the new federal governments wanted to have more control. They made many grants to the states, and with those grants, they told the states what to teach and to whom to teach it to. Actually, the taxes were from the states, and the feds collected them. Then in order to get their money back, the states had to conform to the rules of the feds.

They did this through testing and evaluations, but all states tested for the different things. The states wanted to create their own tests, and the fight went further. When the federal uniformed people came into the schools, the schools became the property of the feds. Too bad!

This was accentuated after the First and the Second World Wars as well as after the Korean and the Vietnam actions.

The second President Bush tried a program called No Child Left Behind. It didn't work well because the slower students began to slow up those who could work faster. Now, worldwide, our nation is left behind.

School districts that were doing well began to slow down; there were no groups of slow schools to reciprocate. We can notice the whole of the districts going backward. The leaders of the slower schools became the state and the federal leaders, and the leaders of the slower schools became more in control. To me, this is a very sad situation.

The programs that allowed the student to work as fast as possible and to help the other students were far more superior to the methods used in this program. After a few years, the program is losing ground when the teachers and the parents realize that all the students are not functioning at the level they were.

Since the citizenry were of mixed languages, it made it necessary to help all children to learn English that was, and still is, the dominate language. English has always been a mixture of other languages, and many foreign words have been accepted as common to our usage.

When the Indians were subdued, some of them lost their culture and were supposed to be integrated into the rest of the communities. It was very hard for them to change from their many habits and cultures; this was finally forgotten and allowed them to be of their own culture. The result of this was that the Indian children were confused. There are some still on their reservations and still sovereign wards of the federal government. This is only right because this was their land, and the foreigners stole it from them. They are a proud people and have complete cultures and should be left to their own culture. Within each group, allow those in charge to be in charge.

Out in the various communities, the schools maintained, and between the parents and the governments, curriculum was set. Since the Constitution gave the rights of education to the states, it worked for a while, but that soon was grabbed by the federal government.

AFTER THE WARS

When the military returned, they were not sure if they wanted to be schoolteachers; some did, and mostly the women continued teaching as they had while the men were overseas. Many of the soldiers wanted to better care for their families and worked the GI Bill to give them administrative or college positions.

It was about this time that the schools got smart and made the students stay in school until at least the eighth grade. Teachers were helped, and the schools were better staffed with the additional help of both men and women.

In the events listed here, we are aware that the teachers did not have the freedom they needed to really educate their students. Little has changed in total, and in many places in the world, leaders will tell the teachers what to teach and not allow the children to explore other venues.

Our new country went on with things as they were for a while. They soon realized it would be necessary to strengthen education for the sake of the children and their future.

Now teachers are getting organized and starting to come to more power, but as this became apparent, certain parties wanted to still control the teachers. New positions were created, and those who suffered the most were the students. Selfish people do not look at the problems they create by inserting their uneducated attitude in the edifices of education.

We have begun to see schools that are sometimes allowed to teach those things that are needed. They are called by charter schools and different names and are guided by the people of the state in order to gain funds from the states and the federal government. Some are sponsored by religions and are allowed to teach things of that religion. Parents are required to help with the financing of the school and allow those things that are taught there. We see growth in most of the students that is superior to those in the public schools. These schools have more care and have the students learn more.

Chapter 5

RESPONSIBILITIES AND ACTIONS FOR THE CHILDREN'S SAKE

While teachers have a responsibility of teaching, so do others. In this chapter, we will discuss these people and the organizations that should help our children to learn and to want to learn. I start with a true event to exemplify that others will listen to what they hear most of, and it will help them to learn and develop their attitudes and habits. Consider your children as the beans in the experiment. Children become what they are taught, and they learn.

When I was a junior in college, two fellow students and I wanted to see what would happen to bean plants if they had music accompanying them while they were growing. We got six pots and five pairs of speakers and made six relatively soundproof boxes with glass fronts. We placed potting soil in each of the pots and planted three beans in each pot.

One of the boxes contained no speakers for a control project. In the second box, we played classical music constantly. In the third box, we piped in popular music from the sixties era, for this was done in the sixties. In the fourth box, we played country and western music. In the fifth box, we played jazz, and in the sixth box, we played rock and roll.

We watered each plant every other day and placed a spotlight in each box that we turned on for ten hours a day. In this way, the only variable was the music or lack of music for each potted plant.

As the plants began to grow, box 1 had a somewhat normal growth and grew to ten inches in the two months of the project. It was very pretty, but in the silent world, the stems were smaller than what we thought should be the normal growth.

Box 2 grew more rapidly, and the leaves were larger and the stems were solid. Within the two months, it was a very beautiful plant with straight and thick stems. The flowers were plentiful, and the plant grew faster than the others.

Box 3 contained growth similar to the silent one. The plant was not as tall, but the stems were stronger. In the two months, it grew no more than the first box.

Box 4 with country western music, not country rock, grew better than 1 and 3, but it was not nearly as beautiful as box 2. In two months, it did have flowers on the plant but not as numerous as box 2.

In box 5, we found the plants growing wildly, not straight but crooked and wandering all over the box. The stems were thin and weak, and after two months, the growth had gone to the plant with no buds anywhere on the plant. The height was only half of the control box 1.

Box 6 was the worst of all. It almost became an uncontrolled vine. The leaves were small, and the stems were all over the box with no control or direction on them.

The reason I bring this up to the parents is because the music and the habits the children gain will control them. There is a direct relationship to the controls given to the children and the plants. Music and literature will be the key to their success and habits in life. I am not saying if they listen to hard rock, they will be duds, but if they listen to classical music, their minds will be more relaxed, and they can learn better.

We have more things today than in the sixties and seventies, more distractions and more things to draw the children away from their studies. When people tell me they let their children make up their own mind, I really understand they are saying they really don't care what their children do, and they allow their peers to teach them what is good and bad. This is a very serious mistake.

All too often, we find young people trying to emulate their parents or older people. They want what they see others have but don't realize the others had to work hard to get what they have, or they got it illegally. Some parents think it to be cute when the five- to ten-year-olds want to act like adults. What is happening here is that they are losing their childhood. We even find this in the schools, but we will discuss that later.

Parents have the responsibility to raise their children better than their parents did. They can ask their parents what they did wrong, and then they don't have to make the same mistakes. Please realize there has been only one person on this earth that made no mistakes, and those around him were jealous and killed him.

We all make mistakes, but it is important that when we realize those mistakes, we rectify and correct them. This is the mark of an adult as, many times, we see kids (and adults) not wanting to take credit for those things they do wrong.

Parents must go to the schools, especially in the elementary years, to help the teachers understand why the kids do what they do in a positive way.

When we teach our children that the teachers are authority and that they must not listen to authority, we are not doing that child or any other child any favor. We are only confusing them. We give them room to become antagonistic toward the school and the teachers.

We must remember that teachers are humans as well and will make mistakes, but so are the parents and others; they also make mistakes. It is very important that the parents do not discuss errors with the children but rather go to the teacher and get understanding and allow that teacher to correct their mistakes if they made mistakes. It would be well if the teacher who felt the parents made mistakes in handling certain situations would do the same. What one person likes, another person may worry about the consequences of those actions. Parents, teachers, and administration personnel should work together and allow no dictators aboard.

There are many people who are responsible for the progress of the child. Here is a short list, even though there are others: parents, teachers, peers, administrators, clergy and other community leaders, the students themselves, and in some cases, the judicial and law enforcement people.

Named in the paragraph above, we must understand the child will learn from each entity listed, and the parents are the only constant that can be counted upon. Teachers change each year, and so do the others in some way or another. If the parents need help, ask for it; if they need help with a teacher, see the administration, and have a conference with the teacher and the administrator. All too often, things that the parents feel are problems can be discussed, and many times, the problems are either because of a misunderstanding or because someone is very out of line. Don't blame others until you can discuss it with that person.

Parents **should** take every opportunity to meet with school officials, and it would be nice for the parent to discuss things that are working as well as those that are not working. Parents are in a partnership with the educators when it comes to their children. We all want what is best for our children; however, some may think one thing is better, and others disagree. That is OK; talk it out, and make an effort to discuss these things so you can come to a good conclusion that will help the child please the teacher and the parents. Think on this please.

Parents are the first line of offense and defense. They know their children best. They need to help them with their homework if possible; if it's not possible, then perhaps that would be something the parent could work on. I will discuss this later and in more detail. Please be patient.

TEACHERS' RESPONSIBILITIES

First, let me state my opinion: teachers are not made into teachers; they have to want to become teachers. I feel the teachers are born to be teachers, and they must be trained to do the best they can, and they must learn methods to be successful.

Children go to school to learn, and it is the responsibility of the teachers to present information to the children that will help them learn. The teachers must teach comprehension so the child will understand what they have been taught. Introduction must be followed up with clear comprehensive instruction at the level the child is learning. To do less than teaching full comprehension is to cause each child to become frustrated and lose interest in school and learning.

Teachers have the obligation to help each child do the best he/she can. The teachers cannot have a favorite nor can they slight a child because of one reason or another. Children have the right to expect they will have the same chance as another. This does not mean that every child will learn in the same way or that they will be on the same page as the other children.

As you were trained as a teacher, you learned that children learn at different rates and in different ways. This is the same as adults. Adults may become frustrated with school if they are not learning as much and as fast as the others in the class. The children are the same.

PEERS' RESPONSIBILITIES

When children start school, they will react to school as they have been taught by the adults in their lives. When the child makes friends at school, they will either copy the actions of their friends, or the friends will copy them, or they will share habits and ideas. If the parents have taught them to like to read and learn and help them to stay on that path to learning and the teacher makes it important, the child will learn and stay on task.

Hopefully, they will become leaders in the class or follow good leaders in their class who want to learn and be in a learning mode. Training will help with this (at home), and hopefully, the parent will be aware of problems. Teacher-parent conferences are very helpful and can be productive.

ADMINISTRATORS' RESPONSIBILITIES

Administrators are very important in the process unless they are only there for the money or the prestige. The principal has the responsibility to learn all the children's names, not only of the very good students and the very bad students, but of all the students. The principals must know what the teachers are working with and how they are doing. Additionally, they should try to learn the names of the parents and which child belongs to whom.

Another necessity is for the principal to have an open door policy for the parents, the teachers, and the students. With this, the secretary must keep track of the meetings of the administrative personnel and the counselors to keep pace with the progress of each parent, teacher, and child in the school. We will discuss this later also.

CLERGY RESPONSIBILITIES

The responsibility of the clergy is to help the parents and the children at their religious meetings and perhaps counsel them, but it is not their responsibility to intercede at school. They can advise the parents what they can do, but the parent has the job of working with the school.

Clergy and other religious people need to help the parents help themselves. They can help better to allow the parents and the children prepare.

OTHER COMMUNITY LEADERS

It is advisable if any community leader wants to help the schools solve problems that they do not become the problem. It is OK to attend the school board meetings and vote for elections, but for them to interfere with the schools is neither appropriate nor acceptable.

Private meetings with the superintendent or the principal or even the teacher can be helpful for understanding, but to try to change the process, one must not overstep their own bounds. Would the mayor like the school leaders to come into the mayor's office and try to change the way things are done? That would also be very inappropriate.

Schools are not closed societies, but they have their own ways to accomplish things, and if everyone tried to inject different methods, it would cause havoc that would not recover, and the children would be the losers.

All too often, people want to run the lives of others without realizing what the repercussions would be. Too many judges, well meaning, have caused problems in the schools by decisions that would be not in the best interest of the schools nor the children. We will discuss this later.

Those in authority pay little attention to the effects on another. They only want their way and seem to never care about others. They must really have an ego that is unimpeachable.

EFFECTS OF OTHER PERSONS ON THE CHILDREN'S LEARNING

Have you, as a parent, a teacher, a friend, or any of the controls ever walked into a situation and made a flash decision, then later have the understanding that it was wrong? All too many will not admit wrongdoing.

In the event one makes a mistake, he/she needs to admit that it was a mistake. When one does think they are right and yet later find out they are wrong, it becomes very necessary to let those around them, especially those directly affected, know that the error will be corrected and straightened out. It takes an intelligent and caring person to own up to their own mistakes. To correct the mistake, even if it is accidental or made in innocence, is the only way the children will learn to own up to their mistakes.

If the child receives help from those they trust (teachers, parents, etc.), they will be more prone to help others. Relationships that teach values may be the only values the child has. The schools can teach some things, but morals and values seem not to be acceptable.

A child is so tender and so innocent when starting school that they want so much to please. They trust, they attempt, and many times, their lives are damaged by uncaring and thankless people. If a child is told he/she is stupid, dumb, ignorant, or incompetent, that will be what that child believes in. They will act out the name called and become exactly what they have been called. Never call other person negative names; actually, this will demean you, and the abused person will not trust you anymore, nor will they be as open as they were previous to their belittlement. If you have reason to berate another, do so in a quiet place, alone with that person, and perhaps with another in authority over you or that person. After your battement, show more concern for that person. I'm not saying that you must be a friend, but praise where praise is earned and needed. Think before you act and listen to the person you are counseling to see if you have made a mistake in your judgment.

PERSONAL EXPERIENCE IN A CLASSROOM

While teaching in a small school district, I encountered a student who was convinced that he was dumb. I taught math and spelling to seventh-grade students, and Don[†] came to me and told me not to expect much from him because he had been told he would never amount to much. Don was

---

[†]   The name is to help conceal Don's real identification.

in my spelling class, and when given a weekly test, he would make funny marks rather than letters. In the first three weeks, he never tried to get one word right.

I called him to my desk and quietly asked why. He said he didn't know how to make letters. For the next three weeks, I excused him from spelling and had him learn to print letters and make small words. He really got into it and worked hard to learn small and short words. At the end of the six-week period, I gave Don a C in spelling. He was happy because that was the first C he had ever **earned** in his life.

The next week was important to him; he wanted to try spelling with the other kids. We made a deal that if he would get all the words right in any of the next six weeks, I would give him an A in spelling. He made it on the fifth week. He actually earned another C, but a promise is a promise, and he was so happy that he ran all the way home to show it to his parents.

For the third six-week period, he had to get two perfect papers in spelling. He made it to the last test. In the fourth period, he had to get three 100-percent papers. Again, he was successful, and he earned a good grade. In the fifth period, he made four 100-percent papers. He gave credit to his parents because they had tested him often. In the sixth week, he knew he would have to have five 100 percents.

He had the following scores: 100, 95, 100, 100, 100, and 95. He was upset with himself, but when the report card came out, he had an A. Then he came to me with tears in his eyes and demanded that I give him the grade he earned. I told him that I did.

I had him add up all the scores and divide them by six and see what grade he received. That totaled to 590, and he divided that by six and got a 96.6. He then realized he had earned an A and worked hard from then on.

Don went on to high school and then to college. He used his math and natural abilities to become an architect. I was happy for him, and he offered to have a house built for me. I told him no. I did what I did for the student, not for my personal gain.

I take little credit for his success. He had to do the work, he had to learn, and his parents helped him. The joy I received was all the reward I wanted.

Attitude is very important in raising children; also, it is very necessary in teaching children. Things that should be in every school are a viable dress code, a verified homework, and a conduct toward peers, teachers, administration, and law enforcement, from and toward the parents and other adults. Additionally, parents and children should have concern for the child, knowing how to act around abusive persons and how to respond to unwanted attention, unwarranted discipline, and treatment by both friends and strangers.

Trained law enforcement instructors should be present and often instructing students and teachers in the matters listed above and, if certain things are brought to them, create material to help the child, the teachers, and the parents understand what to do if.

Scholarship is also important in training a child for future lives. Self-discipline should be part of the child. Not only in learning, in working, and in accomplishing, but also in their daily lives. In the event a child has no self-confidence, he has no or little direction. He has no plans and becomes a wanderer. He needs to be reached as soon as possible so these things will become part of his life and habits. We as adults need to help the child help him-/herself.

Patterned living is what the child learns and will develop. If the parents show self-discipline, courage, willingness to try, and many other things to prepare each child for life, that child will have a better chance of being a productive citizen.

If children see a clean home, a clean classroom and school, and a generally clean habitat, that child will have a need for cleanliness. If the parents, the teachers, and others are polite to and when talking about the other, the children will also have the attitude of politeness in their lives. In the event there are problems, the adults can make appointments and meet without the child if there may be negative attitudes there. Around that child, though, politeness will help the child to be polite.

We are what we do. Our children will be what they see. Learn the rules of the school and try to have some of the same rules in the home. Both the parents and the teachers will influence the children by their actions. It is necessary for each to realize what we are teaching the child and how the child will respond when he sees what we have done.

Parents, please try to dress as if you were going to school, and buy children proper clothing for school. Stay away from the fads; clothing will set the child for life, and he will learn to like what he is allowed to wear. If one child is dressing in a provocative way, that child should be dealt with by a counselor, the school nurse, a gender teacher, or an administrator, and the parents should be called in for this conversation. The child can be present for the first statement through the final decision if the administration will agree to this action; it will help make this a productive meeting. If there was a dress code, the problem would be much easier to handle and easier for the child to get on board.

Teachers go to college to gain knowledge and methods of teaching. When they get a leader, a principal, a superintendent, or a peer who wants them to teach in their fashion, everyone loses, especially the children. Individuality is the key to a good educator. What to teach is for the leaders to decide, but how to teach it is for the teacher to decide. We will all lose if we cannot put our individuality into our teaching. We will soon find that the children will also lose their desire to learn when they realize the teacher is not happy with the way they have to teach. For the whole sixth-grade class to be on page 87 when the individual did not and still does not understand page 50 is ludicrous, and for a child having to go ahead without comprehending what he has been taught is neglect. Negativism is the opposite of learning.

Chapter 6

POLITICS VS. THE SCHOOL SYSTEMS

We began to have a new awareness of the importance of school and gave to the education portion of the country a new respect. With the thought afloat that teacher either knew everything or they should know everything, other entities wanted to gain control over the schools and the educators.

When the air cleared after the wars, we found political unrest, thinking that the schools were wrong. They realized they had not allowed everyone the same rights to an education. They grew aware that there were segregated schools where these wrongs were prevalent. Sometimes, it was caused by the arrogance of the people; sometimes, it was caused by the neighborhood schools, and sometimes, it appeared by design of the school boards. In any case, the schools were segregated, and since the

Constitution states that all men were created equal, all people were allowed to have the same rights as far as education was concerned. It seemed that the best teachers were found in the district that was the most affluent. It seemed that the segregated schools were the poorest families.

The school boards created better buildings for the nonsegregated schools, giving them better chances for the eventual success of the students. These students eventually received a better education and better lives.

For the segregated schools, a fewer number of students finished high school and went on to college. The homes were not as affluent as in the nonsegregated schools, and the children had very low self-esteem and poorer chances of success. It is basically still the same way but not always the school's fault.

There were many ways to solve this problem. The federal courts decided they would solve the problem. They could only come up with a sudden change in all the various school districts. Transporting children from one neighborhood to another seemed to be the easiest fix. We have to know (in hindsight) this was not the best solution. The children were now in areas they were not familiar with; many friends were not transferred to the same schools, and there was general confusion. Actually, when the federal government tries to repair things and have control, it never succeeds.

Laws were created, rules were set, grants were given to the schools that complied with the law, and federal troops were sent to the schools that resisted. Under this same principle, housing rules were changed, and many other laws were enacted. For a system that had been in process for many years, the Congress and the judiciary as well as the president wanted it to happen yesterday. It is hard to change all things at once, and the people needed to be sold on the program. Force made the process last for more than twenty years, and it still isn't complete.

Common sense would say that when one hurries, too many mistakes are made. The old proverb says, "Haste makes waste." With these three simple words and with so much time to accomplish their tasks to change the minds and the actions of the people, the rush to judgment and action actually slowed the whole process. This author realizes the desegregation of the schools was necessary, but one that would not have been so hard on the population would have been as follows:

Year 1: Desegregate grades K-3.
Each year, add one grade 4, 5, 6, 7, and 8.
After six years, add two grades per year, totaling eight years for all classes

—

until all the local schools are completely integrated.

It would also be necessary to bring on board all the parents. Those parents, who live in the poorest areas, usually did not finish school and need to catch up with the others.

In the first chapter, we discussed having the parents return to the schools and, if they were behind their own children in education, have night classes or other classes to help the parents learn the importance of what an education means. This will give those parents a desire to help their children gain a better life for them than they (the parents) were able to get. It would raise the standard of living and make our world a much better place to rear our children. When a person feels like the bottom of society, that is what they will become. We must **_ALL_** help others succeed, or we will all fail.

During this process, upgrade the knowledge of the affected teachers. Help the principals learn to share their knowledge with the other schools. It is important that we not only update the children but also the staff.

When the schools were segregated, the teachers were usually paid more in the nonsegregated schools and were able to update their methods and knowledge, and for a teacher to move to the segregated school, he/she would not, for the most part, be able to progress as well. The pay to the segregated schools was less, thus giving the teachers the need to stay with the money. The schools that were segregated were in poorer shape, and the school board members wanted it to stay that way.

When the desegregation of the schools happened, all of a sudden, people began to realize the segregated schools were in poorer shape than the nonsegregated schools. Many people wanted this rectified now. In this battle, there were many sides.

All too often, people wear blinders and do not care who gets hurt until the hurt is upon them. They seem to think everyone should think and act like they do, and then everything would be OK. Think on something else: "If everyone thought the same way, everyone would want the same girl or the same man. They would not be able to see any variety in their lives." We have to realize that teachers teach in different ways, and children learn in different ways. They cannot all be on the same page at the same time and learn the same things. Each individual will do the best they can, but some go faster, and some go slower.

The NEA (National Education Association) gave this assessment when it wrote about the so-called No Child Left Behind Law. They first stated that **<u>One size does not fit all.</u>**

Every child can learn, but parents and teachers know that every child can't learn at the same speed or in the same way.

The so-called "No Child Left Behind" law forces a one-size-fits-all approach on children, regardless of their individual differences and needs.

This law demands that all children meet the same level of achievement in the same amount of time, regardless of their individual differences and needs.

This law reduces kids to a test score by relying *exclusively* on standardized tests to measure progress—tests that simply ignore all the circumstances, both inside and outside the classroom that can affect a child's ability to learn.

This law forces teachers to teach to the test, instead of giving children the individual attention they need.

Who gave those in Washington the ability and knowledge to know what is best for all children and adults? How many of them are teachers and were successful in the classroom? How many of them struggled with their own studies?

Many years ago, people were enamored with the IQ tests. Upon looking closely, they discovered the tests were flawed. The flaw was forcing everyone to take the same tests. The tests were made by and for people in certain areas, discounting those in the fringes like in the poorer parts of the United States and on the farms and any special areas. It also discounted those of different races and different backgrounds; this was shown by the questions that counted on different attitudes and skills. It is an impossible task to account for all the differences in the people in the United States as well as in the other countries.

We, at that time, had people from different countries that had no skill in English and the colloquial differences of the minorities. We were all supposed to be part of the bright suburbs, and others had not developed in the same class. Really, this is still the same, and no understanding is shown.

The wealth of the parents was very important in gaining the IQ of the child. How much time was spent in the learning of the child at home? How many times did the parents visit the school, and how much education did the parents actually achieved? The books that were available to the children, the music they listened to, and if or not they attended any religious functions—all these items and more were involved with the knowledge the kids had.

When something new was tried in the schools, (1) Did the parents know about it, and were they brought up to the new ideas? (2) Did the people in the community know anything about the changes? (3) Did the schools attempt to teach the new ideas to the parents through the PTA or some other organization?

I recall in the 1960s a new math program. It was called Modern Math. Since I understood math easily, it was not a problem for me. However, the parents were lost. I found at a book sale a book entitled *Modern Math*, but it had the copyright date of 1867. I realized that schools were in a magic cycle in teaching probably every subject. Each time it is reintroduced, more is added to it, and the knowledge of that generation will have a more knowledgeable understanding than the past generations.

In light of this, those who are trying to leave no child behind are trying to accelerate this process. The only thing wrong with this is that in the past, we were taught with comprehension and not by osmoses, or seemingly through that process, the children would learn.

Politics needs to stick to the law and not try to make changes in the educational processes of the children. The United States used to have the best schools in the world; if we are lucky now, we are seventeenth or eighteenth in the world now. The people in the schools know how to fix this; the politicians know how to make it worse.

With the way the teachers are expected to accomplish things, they should have law degrees, medical degrees, law enforcement training, and many other abilities. These things do not equate to EDUCATION. Organizations should have to go through the school board, the superintendent, and the principal with a copy explaining what they want to introduce to the children. The teachers and the parents should be brought in to discuss this stuff before it is introduced to the school children en masse. It is important that if the parents do not like this stuff, their children should be exempted from receiving it or hearing about it. If a meeting is called for interested children, it should be off campus with a note from their parents, or allow the parents to come to the meeting. This should be the only way these things should happen. All too often, school personnel get the feeling that they are the school, and they can do no wrong. After being an educator for forty-five years, I know that I have made mistakes and that every teacher I know has made mistakes as well as the principals, the superintendents, and even the school boards. We will discuss this later in the book.

Chapter 7

DISCIPLINE AND ITS INVOLVEMENT IN THE EDUCATION PROCESS

Discipline is defined as the following: "Training that is expected to produce moral or mental improvement" and "punishment that is expected to instruct or train." In other words, teaching by using discipline is to "teach, instruct, correct and to train and if necessary to punish."

There are times that there can be no instruction by the teachers or learning by the students due to the misbehavior of some of the students. In the event the teacher orders the child to go to the principal's office, about half of the time, that student will go somewhere else. In those cases, the child feels he has gotten away with his bad behavior and will use this as a method of getting out of school.

There are much better solutions to this kind of behavior. I will mention only a few and allow your minds to think of others.

Teachers should have a phone in their classroom and be able to call the parents soon after the moment of the infraction. The child should speak to their parent and tell their side; this will allow the parent to see what is going on. In the event the child lies, the teacher will know of it, and that teacher can ask the parent to come to school. This way would involve time from the class but also allow the class to hear the whole exchange.

The child should take a note home, and the teacher would have to call to make sure the note gets home. If it doesn't get home or if it doesn't get back to the teacher, there should be a conference with the parents to assist in trying to get the child back on course.

If either of these scenarios is effective, we can be glad. In the event they don't work, perhaps the parents and the teacher can come up with a solution. There are many ways to solve the problems, but the courts have stopped some of these ways. This was due to the overuse of the same methods. Rather than punish the teacher or counsel them, the courts decided corporal punishment was out. Probably this was because some of the judges received paddles when they were in school.

We cannot send the child home because the school is responsible for them until they arrive at their home. Parents and teachers should get together prior to the bad acts at the school, say in a PTA meeting or some such forum. The education of each child is so important that we cannot leave any out. If the child does not want to go to public school and can't afford private, perhaps it will be necessary to send that child to a school for that type of student. Maybe the child wants to earn money, so half-schooling could be worked out.

With the importance of discipline and the abuse by some teachers, the courts became involved. Rather than disciplining the abusive teachers, the courts said that the use of corporal punishment will no longer be acceptable. This is a remnant of the Wild West: when an Indian killed a white man or a white man killed an Indian, those in the group of the murdered person would take revenge, not on the culprits, but on the easiest prey available. Rather than prosecute the guilty, others were attacked and killed—in many cases, women and children.

The judiciary and the other politicians decided they didn't care about the classroom of children who will lose days of learning, but that the child, who knowingly disrupted the school, should not receive the available punishment as a last result. In my forty-plus years in education, I have seen the classroom become a very unpleasant place; teachers who try to control the class are either berated or fired. There has to be a meeting of the minds; do the judges want the educational level of the schools in the United States to continue its downward slide, or do they want the educators to again have the necessary control of the classroom for healthy and productive learning and teaching?

There are too many people who want to be effective in the schools and who want to control the schools. With the courts and other self-serving groups desiring their projects to be in the schools, our schools have become very inadequate and will continue on this path until discipline is restored. Though discipline is the most important, there are other events that have come under the scrutiny of others when they want the schools to become parents without any authority, and neither the parents know the teachers and vice versa.

The chief of these is called sex education. Education means that all avenues on both sides of the issues be brought to the forefront so a person hearing these different sides can make an informed choice in their lives. The children are taught the sex acts and how to do these things "safely." There is no responsibility training, no care for the results of the act, and no moral training, which in fact, without that morality, may give the child the idea that it is not a moral issue.

When an adult or an older person thinks they can accomplish certain things with the children, the thought may be that the children are expendable and are there for that predator. When a young lady or, even in this day, a young man is alone, the thought may be that they are free for the taking. This is as animalistic as any other behavior, and animals don't bother the young ones other than to eat them in some animal societies.

Now since the courts have gotten into education, let us also get into the court system on how to stop these predators. If a child is killed, it should require the death penalty. If a person is attacked, raped (under the age of consent is statutory rape), and is very bothered about the situation, the perp should be locked up until the victim regains their normal state. If the victim dies or becomes unstable, the perp should also be locked up for the rest of his/her life. Rape and incest cannot have a statute of limitations. It's like any other serious crime should be open until it is closed, as long as proof is there for the assault and the rape.

Parents, church leaders, doctors, and other responsible people are good resources for sex education. It is not a subject for the schools. I have heard kids say, after the sessions, that we have got homework in this class. It is absurd that the morality and the responsibility of the kids have not been taught.

When I was in school, there were very few teen-parents. When my children were growing up, there were more teenage mothers in the schools, mainly due to the SEX EDUCATION classes in the schools. Now when my grandkids are married, teen parents is in the epidemic stage, and many want nothing to do with the babies. They either kill them or give them away. Think about what has happened in our country. In other countries, it is more rampant.

We have safeguards in the schools that mandate teachers and educator employees to contact authorities if we feel the child has been mistreated. We turn this information over to the authorities and hardly ever know what has happened. Why is there not a law and responsibility of the parents and teachers that when a child is hurt, raped, or molested by their peers, this also can be turned over to the authorities? It used to be that when an eighteen-year-old has been raped, the perp gets a mandatory jail sentence. They then dropped it to sixteen years old and called it statutory rape, but now, even that law is forgotten as long as the child agreed to it. It is still statutory rape unless the law is changed and unless the perp is as young as the victim. It still is rape, but on both sides of the case. They are too young and do not have the proper emotional comprehension to be able to make that choice. Please consider this. Schools are now having special classes for pregnant girls, but the boys are absent.

In some states, there are police officers given an office in the schools to assist with the lawbreakers. This is a step in the right direction, but parents should also be more visible in the schools. We will discuss this in the last chapters and give one way for a solution. There are others, but I will not go into them because the water would be muddied with so many methods.

The school board is the elected body that should ascertain the habits of the teachers prior to hiring them. There is a personnel department who should be in charge of making these findings. Better and more experienced teachers should receive better and more rewards. We will also discuss this later.

The only place we should find politics in the schools is in the social studies classes. Teachers can show the students the methods of the courts, the law enforcement, and the prisons. Field trips would be good for them. These same students should elect their own leaders in the school and have a mock election for the local, county, state, and federal leaders. They should study their rhetoric and make a firm choice by what they think. Teachers should not interfere with the choices of the children as long as these choices are legal.

In the way the teachers are expected to accomplish things, they should have law degrees, medical degrees, law enforcement training, and many other abilities. These things do not equate to EDUCATION.

Organizations should have to go through the school board, the superintendent, and the principal with a copy of the printout they want the children to receive. The parent organization should be involved and know what their children are receiving, and then maybe a paper can be passed out, inviting the children and the parents to come to a meeting off campus. That is the only way.

Chapter 8

DISCOVERING AND USING THE VARIOUS LEARNING PROCESSES

People learn in different ways. We could discuss tactile and other methods, but rather, let's use common terms that all can understand.

<u>VISION LEARNING</u>

If a person is learning through their vision, they will use their eyes. This will include reading, writing, and watching. It does not, however, include working with the hands, the sense of smell, and in some ways, the hearing. These are the people who can learn how to do something by reading about it. They can watch the process on TV or hear about in on a tape. Their minds will create pictures for them, and they can visualize those things they need in order to learn.

HANDS-ON LEARNING

Some people will need to try things themselves and cannot visualize the process without actually doing the process. Good mechanics mostly learn this way. They can be shown in a book, on film, on TV, or verbally, but they do not really understand until they do it themselves. Many times, people learn to cook in this manner.

TRIAL AND ERROR

Some people cannot be told how to do things. They have to try and fail. Some think they are hardheaded, but mostly, they only comprehend processes by actually making mistakes of trying. They cannot get the picture in their minds and therefore can say they understand and still make mistakes.

In all these processes, those who learn in a different manner will become frustrated when another cannot do what they think they should. They will learn to write, read, and calculate by actually doing it; they can place the method right beside their work and still not copy the problem. Patience is a virtue, and it needs to be exercised by the teachers. Many people call these people slow learners, but they are doing the best they can.

The different ways of learning should be discovered by the teachers and the parents as early as possible. Both of these groups should communicate their findings with each other. After all, it is the child's life we are helping or destroying. We cannot put them back in the corner and forget them. Most everyone can learn—some faster, some slower, and others, somewhere in between.

We cannot expect all children to be on page 99 at the same time. This is why our reading teachers have so many groups. There are all different types of learners in each reading groups, so these groups can help one another.

A child will act out if comprehension is hard to find. The peers know how to speak the language the actor needs. Sometimes, a child will be way ahead of others and be completely bored with having to be as slow as the other class members. This was the problem Einstein had; only, he was ahead of even the teachers.

In one of the schools, I taught math to junior high kids. I realized these children were not at the same level that many thought seventh-grade students would be. I reviewed the entire math they had up to that point for two weeks. I then gave them a generic test that would tell me where they were.

I had thirty-nine kids in six different classes and had 236 different levels of learning. I created packets, starting with making and understanding numbers through algebra. I interviewed each child and gave them books with the material they understood to work on. I had to procure books from first grade to sophomore levels. I allowed them to make covers so others would not know where each student was working on.

I talked to some of the algebra students and had them help others as peer trainers. There was one girl I had to help. She could not even make the numbers. She had been passed from grade to grade because of her age. You could take a ruler and place it on her forehead, and it would touch her chin and barely touch the end of her nose. Her face was concave, and the other teachers had placed her in the back of the room and let her sit there. She had no friends, and some of the kids tried to tease her. I did not allow this and threatened severe punishment if it happened again. It stopped.

I made dotted lines in the form of numbers and allowed her to trace them. I taught her the value of the numbers and their names. Soon, I was able to teach her to add, then to subtract, then to multiply, and finally, after two years, how to divide. She had to pass each level by getting 80 percent correct just like the other children. She learned to read math words and symbols. We worked for her, and she was able to keep up with the various classes. She finally passed division by dividing two digits into four digits successfully. Her mother would come to class to help her, and actually, it helped her mother as well.

This young lady proved to herself she wasn't dumb and that she could learn. Though she quit school during her freshman year, she learned to read and write by her mother's help. She had a much better life.

It is very important that parents involve themselves with the learning of their children. It is not only the schools that teach children but it is everyone that the child comes in contact with. Incidentally, I gave her an A for her work in my class. She deserved it and was very proud of the work she had done in the seventh and eighth grades. She learned and was not passed on because of her age. Her self-esteem was raised, and she was a better person for it.

My second experience was in a small school in south-central Arizona. In this school, they had decided the kindergarten and the first-grade teachers would judge the abilities of the children and place them in high, low, or medium classes according to their educational achievement. This was bad for many reasons. The most important reason is that the

late bloomers had no chance to move up unless this was approved by the committee.

One student came to my class with the idea that he could not learn. He had been placed in the low class in the first grade, and there, he stayed. I was teaching math for seventh and eighth graders and one class of spelling. This student came into the spelling class in the seventh grade. I would teach the twenty words at the first of the week and work on those words until the test on Friday. In the first two weeks of school, Sam—let's call him by this name—only made funny squiggles on the paper by the numbers. After the second week of complete failure, I challenged Sam to study. I wanted him to do the prep work for the week and learn the words.

He responded to this by spelling half of the words correctly but not attempting the rest of them in the third week. We had another conversation, and I told him he was doing fine, but ten words were not enough.

In the fourth week, he got fourteen words correct. I was happy and gave him the earned C for the week. In the fifth week, he completed sixteen words correctly. And in the sixth week, he only missed one word. This was a review of the other five weeks, and he knew what he needed to do.

Receiving a C on his report card, he was happy. It was the first C he had ever earned.

—

When he came into my class on the following Monday, he asked what he had to do to get an A. That was easy; he had to try every week, but during one week, he had to get a perfect paper—a 100 percent. The rest, he had to try on and get as well as he could.

He worked hard and made his hundred on the fifth week. He got his A and was happy. He asked if the same deal was on for the next six weeks, and I told him with one change. He had to get two perfect papers. For the fourth six weeks, he had to get three perfect papers, and for the fifth six weeks, he had to get four perfect papers. Finally, he knew that in the last six-week period, he had to have five perfect papers.

He missed one word in the first week. He was perfect on the next four weeks. On the sixth week, he again missed one word. He was angry with himself. But on his report card, he still received his A. He was then angry with me. He didn't want me to give him anymore. I explained to him that he had earned the A. If he would get the average of 95, 100, 100, 100, 100, and 95, he would have the total points of 590 that, divided by 6, gave him a 97 for the final grade. Again, he earned the A. It was not a gift.

He left the school, running as hard as he could. He had been having his mother give him the words at home, and he told her, "Mom, we got an A without having five one hundreds." She told me he then wrote down the scores as I had shown him, and she was amazed he could find the average. He was still failing math.

The next year, he was assigned to my math class, and I helped him to improve his math, his reading, and his many other skills. He, having received success in one area, knew he could succeed in other areas.

Today, Sam is an architect because he learned to believe in himself and to trust his parents and me that he wasn't dumb. To this day, I am very bothered when a kid says he/she is dumb. Everyone can learn. Everyone can improve. The speed of this improvement is in direct comparison to the self-esteem and self-worth that child has in his/her own abilities. Learning is an individual process and is up mainly to the child, but in a close second, we find the parents, the teachers, and those around that child.

When the child sees a particular behavior among adults, they will repeat that behavior. We are all in the sights and the sounds of the children of our world. We are all teachers and all students. We teach more by our actions and behavior than we do by our words. All too often, adults don't allow the child to have an opinion, but rather, they want the children around them to have their (the adults') opinions. We sometimes cause our children to misbehave by not teaching them the way to react with other people. Additionally, each child must learn to respect the adults, to think on what is being said and done, and to learn to treat others the way they want to be treated.

ALL STUDENTS CAN LEARN AND SUCCEED, BUT NOT ON THE SAME DAY IN THE SAME WAY.

—William G. Spady

Chapter 9

MENTALLY CHALLENGED

MENTALLY CHALLENGED children and adults are often treated in very abusive ways. Understandably, they have a problem that is different, but in reality, they are still human beings, and they have needs and will be able to be taught if the proper methods are used. Special teachers are important, and the parents really need to be involved in the learning process.

Who has the responsibility of working for the mentally challenged? Why should they be helped? How can they be helped? What will happen if everyone gives up? Do these people have emotions? Can they cry? Can they be hurt mentally and physically? Let's discuss these things.

WHO IS RESPONSIBLE FOR WORKING WITH THE MENTALLY CHALLENGED?

This, in reality, is the easiest question to answer: basically anyone who comes in contact with one who is mentally challenged. This includes parents, siblings, peers, extended family, teachers, administrators, federal and state government officials, the bus driver, and many more staff. I am sure the minister or leader of their church group would also have responsibility as well.

The mentally challenged did not choose to have deficiencies nor knowingly did the parents. These people can only accept the challenge or reject it. When the person is introduced into society, then society accepts the challenge and will aid not only the person but also the parents. Actually, think on this: if we ignore the opportunity, we will be missing a great opportunity for our own self-growth.

WHY SHOULD THEY BE HELPED?

A person with a handicap, as mentioned previously, did not request it. I remember in *Forrest Gump* when he stated that "Life is like a box of chocolates, You never know what you're gonna get." If we can remember this, we will be happier working with these handicapped people, children or otherwise.

It is important to treat them as close to normal as possible. We know they have a problem and, to an extent, will always have that problem. We do not want to be the type that will hurt them by saying unkind things about them—to their faces or at their backs. This makes us even worse than they are in that we know better.

I like to see children who allow these people in their games even if they will cause them to get behind in scoring; actually, this will place them far ahead of others who don't try.

While working at a school the other day, I noticed a young man walking into the gym, going into the dressing room, and changing into his sports clothing. I watched as when they were divided into different groups, he was one of the first chosen. He was unable to dribble the basketball, but he was a member of the team.

In the event he missed his shot, whoever caught the ball would give him another chance, no matter which team they were on. He would be given three chances, and then the game would continue until he again caught the ball.

When the period was over, his teammates patted him on the back and mentioned how many points he had made for his team. This young man had a lot of trouble walking and had no chance of running, and therefore, he could not dribble. My eyes filled with tears, and my heart raced to see these eighth graders treat a friend that way.

Nothing was spoken about the incident, and I could not bring myself to say anything to any of the children. I only shook the hands of every player and stated "Good game."

I wondered how many adults would have the same patience as these kids. I will always remember that young boy's smile and the happiness of the whole group and hope I can learn something from it.

HOW CAN THEY BE HELPED?

The aforementioned story is only one way. I remember when I was teaching in a large prison in California of a young man (a staff) who had one leg cut off in a farming accident. I befriended him, and we often ate lunch together. Many were the times when I would get up, grab his crutches, and walk off with them in my hand. As soon as he noticed, he would stand up on his leg and hop after me, catching me quickly. One time, a person saw what had aspired and told me I was cruel for taking the crutch. He then turned to my friend and asked if he expected an apology from me.

I will always remember his answer. "No, he is the only one around here that accepts me the way I am. Actually, I am happy he does it once in a while so I know that I have a true friend."

From that time on, no one questioned my act. In fact, there were others who tried, but he always caught them when they took the crutches. My little prank was seen by him as an act of kindness and understanding. This is why I am proud to call him a friend and will always remember him.

There are other ways to show the person he/she is accepted. Ask if you could help push their wheelchair. Pick up something for them at the store, but be sure to ask what they want. In all, there are many more ways to accept these people and let them know that you would be friendly. If a person is mentally slow, be careful and develop a friendship before you tease them. Let them know this is one way you show caring and understanding.

WHAT WILL HAPPEN IF EVERYONE GIVES UP?

The person will be sad for a while, but they will go on and be actually stronger now that they are more on their own. In retrospect, you will be the loser unless you talk to them and, in terms they can comprehend, explain what is going on in your life. I'd bet they will offer to help you as well.

There are some people in this world who only want to be criminals and will never be productive. They may be challenged, or they may have been taught they can better survive being with the criminal element. We must never consider that a person who is mentally or physically challenged is a criminal. We would be fooling ourselves because these people will be as good a citizen as they are taught to be. They may make mistakes, but they will be repentant and will wish to make it up if they can.

DO THESE PEOPLE HAVE EMOTIONS? CAN THEY CRY? CAN THEY BE HURT MENTALLY AND PHYSICALLY?

The federal government has taken it upon themselves to collect taxes and give it back to the states to cover the expenses for the mentally handicapped. Depending upon the severity of their problem, we should integrate these handicapped children and adults into life so they can know what is expected of them in society. This is one of those times when the federal government should turn over the whole amount to the states, earmarked for the mentally challenged. We should hopefully trust the state leaderships to treat these handicapped fairly. If not, then get rid of the leaders.

Generally, the handicapped people will not cry in public. They will wait until they are in comfortable conditions before they let it out. This takes care of the mental part of the questions. If they are hurt physically, it will be much like anyone else. They will cry for sympathy, for anger, and for the actual hurt. Like any other child, it would be cruel to make them cry, and the recipient will lose respect for the one/s who mistreat them.

It is imperative that we realize the learning process of an individual. The handicapped person may be a very late bloomer, and we should be hoping for that time. We all know that Einstein was smarter than his teachers and was frustrated when he couldn't go ahead.

When we work with the handicapped, we must be aware of their progress, small as it may be, and be alerted when they start blooming.

Often, a person will do something that is in their head, and it won't come out right; if we look hard enough, we will be able to see what he/she is trying to do. Assist them and allow them to be inventive and productive. Don't handicap their progress and hope for them to awaken. It may not happen, but then again, it may.

Advice and concern should be as it is now with parents, teachers, psychologists, and others who have a direct interest in the child. Areas of concern should be developed and acted upon by all concerned persons with direction from the teacher and the parents.

We discovered, in one district where I taught, that the teachers in the kindergarten and the first grades would recommend the placement of each child. Interested, I checked on over five hundred children in the past years and found that only three of these children were able to change their level. They grouped the children in mainly three groups: The highest level had those working above their age level. The middle group had those who worked at their age level, and all that were left were placed in the "dumb" group, as the kids would call it. In chapter 2, I told you an experience with one of these children.

We cannot cease to be diligent in involving the children in decisions that may influence their lives in the future. Teachers and parents have a great insight and understanding of the possible progress of the child, and they need to work together to help each child. When discussions are made, it would be appropriate for the child to be in the meeting if both the parent and the teacher agree. This will assist the child in knowing how hard they are working to make them productive. Of course, we should not have them present if there are disagreements and perhaps bad feelings present.

When we all realize that a child is a child, we are all born; at that point, we had very little knowledge. The more the parents help the child, the better off the child will be. We are not trying to imply that the parent can completely cure the mentally challenged child, but they can help their child have a better life. Love is the key to any success in helping the child to succeed in his/her own element. Some parents have the idea that their child is hopeless and will never learn. If they maintain that attitude, it will become a self-fulfilling prophecy. The child can succeed to be his/her best if he/she has support and is taught to try. Losers cannot be winners unless they are taught to be winners. Let us all hope that each child will reach his/her full potential.

Chapter 10

THINGS THAT NEED TO BE CHANGED

Some of the things that need to be changed about public educators are discussed here. In the previous chapters, we have hinted at some of those things that can be corrected and could be changed; education is an entity unto itself, not above any program, definitely not to be made light by any other program. We are teaching the future leaders of our country: your children. We appreciate other parts of society and hope for the same respect from those parts. Some teachers may make mistakes—some accidental, some on purpose. Let the chips fall where they may; if they break the law, they should be punished in some manner or another according to the law, like any other citizen.

During this short book, we have written about different aspects of education in differing modes and means. We now would like to discuss some of these things that we consider paramount to change for the good of the children.

Outside Interference

We have continually talked about the court's involvement in the schools and the laws and regulations they have handed down. We have discussed discipline, what is known as politically correct, private or public outcries that have taken up valuable learning time, unprepared teachers, organizations desiring to have a place in the school, and some other minor things that we may discuss.

Discipline

Unless some of the laws are changed and some of the judicial meddling is softened, the school will become a battleground. Even the felons in prison realize education is important, so the gangs relax their fights in the school settings. They do not want to disrupt those inmates who are trying to better their education. In the public school, the disruptive ones are the ones who are catered to. It is sad that so many people allow the idiom "The squeaky wheel gets the grease" to become the rule rather than the exception.

If a person creates disturbing acts in the school, they should be treated just like anyone on the outside of the schools; they should be taken into custody and learn that this type of behavior is not acceptable. We lament that we cannot use corporal punishment; due to the abuse of a few teachers, this form of punishment has been outlawed. There are some teachers who will, under the guise of frustration, use the most severe form of punishment available. Perhaps we should do like Congress and have a meeting to decide the fate of the child, though this may not sound outrageous; it is.

There are methods of punishment that are almost as effective, and mostly, they work. We can restrict them, give them time off to think about their actions, make them do "busy work," or many other things. Though effective to some, other "tough guys" will only scoff at this attempt.

Dares are one of the things that most parents understand; however, those who do the daring are not the ones that are punished when the other gets caught. Also, in this day, the dares are much more subtle than the simple "I dare you." The adult may remember, in their youth, that some of the children will think their world has come to the end if certain bullies are not satisfied. The little guys always get caught.

Politically Correct

Children in certain areas of the United States don't understand the things that never affect their lives. In the areas of a two-room schoolhouse and even in smaller districts, the things that are supposedly correct seem wrong or, worse yet, are not understood in their world. We need not to disturb our children about adult attitudes and concerns when the children have not encountered these things. We will not take the time here to discuss these things, but we will list some of them: (1) Sex education in the schools, especially in the elementary grades; (2) Women's liberation in the elementary and middle schools; (3) Renaming the Christmas holidays; (4) Gun control; and (5) Racial inequity (in some areas in the United States, it is not a problem; surprise, everyone is treated the same), just to name a few. Everyone is not in the same boat, and everyone does not like the same things, nor should they. We used to tell the children to be their own person, be kind to everyone, and to notice some are different; this is good, and everyone still needs to be treated the same. Now we tell the children that everyone is the same, and this only causes the child to wonder about the visual differences, and they get somewhat confused.

There are so many things that cause disturbances that we would like all schools to be continually upset with. Children do not learn well when they are upset. All too often, people want the solution to be NOW, and they are not willing to fix it, without causing a big ruckus. Do these things belong in the school? Ask yourselves and get your own answers.

I remember a time in a small school district in the fifth grade. The teacher had lined the children up for lunch. They were allowed to line up by their friends they would eat with. All of a sudden, there were three ladies at the door, telling the children to line up in an alternating girl, boy fashion. When the children asked why, the ladies answered, "So you will know there is no difference between boys and girls." One tough little girl stepped forward and told the ladies the difference between boys and girls and spared no words and hoped the ladies would realize the differences. The ladies got angry and went to the principal to complain.

The teacher was called to the principal's office and asked why the child said what she said. He could only answer that the ladies were talking to the children, and the little girl answered her statement. She did not ask to speak nor did she wait for any permission to talk. By these actions, the ladies never returned to that classroom as they couldn't feel welcome. The principal recommended the teacher counsel with the little girl. He never did.

When they arrived at the lunchroom and the other kids saw that the other classes were not segregated but everyone was with their friends, they quickly and quietly changed their positions. Their teachers, if they noticed, did not try to change them back to the lineup that was caused by those ladies. The experiment didn't succeed in that school. The teacher welcomed the "guff," and the kids were happy. Nothing more was said about it for the rest of the year.

Unprepared Teachers

Most of the teachers are prepared well; however, this could be done better. When a person wants to be an engineer, he/she is placed in a locked schedule. When a person wants to be a teacher, they are given a general education for the first two years and then placed on the track for a teacher. If the prospective teacher is lucky, they will get into a classroom in their junior year. This change needs to be effected **NOW!** I recommend teaching classes should begin in the freshman year. They should visit classrooms at least six times in the freshman year, twelve times in the sophomore year, nine weeks in the junior year, and one semester in the senior year. In the junior and senior years, they should be involved in actually teaching subject matter and in the area of their choice.

I had a friend who had been in the engineering track. In his junior year, he realized he would not make it in engineering. He decided to be a math teacher. He had a lot of math in the engineering classes and felt he could make it there. Education was a second choice. When finishing his college, he became a teacher only to find out he was miserable. He took more classes and worked in high school then tried community college. He only found disappointment, and the fact that he didn't like kids didn't make it any easier. He found out that he had no natural abilities in teaching and couldn't get his mind on the subject matter sufficient to explain it to others.

I have found that teachers either have a profound love of teaching others or that they may learn those things, but in the end, without this knack, they will struggle and the kids will lose out. To be a teacher for the pay is also a mistake, for the job that is done, we are the lowest-paid people in our society. We are preparing the children to succeed in life. Without this education, we would all be at the back, planting with a horse, pulling the plow. There would be no possibility of our becoming an upstanding citizen without some education. More than 60 percent of the inmates in the California state prisons have less than a sixth-grade education.

Educated Leaders

If all schools were run by educated people, there would be more education happening. It is understood there has to be a school board, which is filled by interested local people. They should have budget, personnel control, and assurance that the calendars are up-to-date; however, all other jurisdictions should be joint actions with the administration and the board.

As for the organizations who are trying to have a place in the schools, they need to realize education is more important to the children than their special interest. They could have papers passed out to the children addressed to the parents who would have the opportunity to hear what these groups want them to hear, and then the children can make up their minds, with the help of the parents, if they wanted to hear the material or not. In this way, the child would still be taught what the parents want them to hear and not what is given to them in the classroom by nonteachers. A minority group cannot use the schools to push their programs upon the children, the parents, and the others in the area.

When there is a direction the staff should go and a plan to get there, there is a greater chance of success. Personal opinions have no place in schools unless those opinions are founded on facts that can make life better for ALL. It would be better for all children to be equal at school, not in brain power, but in dress, manners, and attitudes. There is not one person better than another unless the second person puts him/herself down by action or inaction. Love, in the sense of caring for each other, is necessary for the good of society.

IMAGINATION IS MORE IMPORTANT THAN KNOWLEDGE.

—Albert Einstein

Epilogue

Preparation for writing this material was a great deal of fun for me as a principal at that time. I went to the PTA meeting at the beginning of the first year and made a list of those parents who would like to create a new system of education. I only had one mother volunteer.

My next venue was with my teachers and other staff, and this time, the response was much greater. There were twelve interested persons. Interestingly, of those twelve, seven were parents within my school.

Those who volunteered were asked to recruit others. The staff and teachers and the single parent went to work, and there were over thirty-six in total. This was great for the purpose of the meeting.

Our first meeting came, and the question was asked: How can we improve the education of our children? I asked the group to discuss this in small groups to answer and fill out the questionnaire and write their answers. I told them this was a brainstorming situation, so all ideas were good. No matter how silly it might sound, it was necessary to express their ideas.

They worked together for an hour, and they had a long list of ways. I next asked them to take a week and go over the list individually for the group they worked in. This time, think on how to accomplish each task, and put together those that fit together. Our next meeting would be to unite all lists and to work out methods to accomplish our main task. They all seemed to be excited.

We put these things together, and the following material is our interpretation of what was discussed. Read the following and make your own ideas known to others. Our schools are in very bad shape and are getting worse every year. Please enjoy yourselves.

THE ROAD NOT TAKEN

Two roads diverged in a yellow wood,
And sorry I could not travel both
And be one traveler, long I stood
And looked down as far as I could
To where it bent in the undergrowth;

Then took the other, as just as fair,
And having perhaps the better claim,
Because it was grassy and wanted wear;
Though as for that, the passing there
Had worn them really about the same,

And both that morning equally lay
In leaves no step had trodden black,
Oh, I kept the first for another day!
Yet knowing how way leads on to way,
I doubted if I should ever come back.

I shall be telling this with a sigh
Somewhere ages and ages hence:
Two roads diverged in a wood, and I—
I took the one less traveled by,
And that had made all the difference.

(Robert Frost, 1874-1963)

Afterword

We have spoken here in the form of a paradigm. For the ones who don't know the word, simply speaking, it is another way of looking at a problem. It is very necessary to have a replacement for the things that have been altered, and in order to do that, it is very necessary to consider very strongly any offering we may have.

We must first find things that are possible and not so far out of the ordinary; people will look at the process and reserve judgment until they can get the whole story down. I have been present where there is a mandated presence required by at least one parent in a family.

Those who have been part of this experiment have found it to be exciting and productive. Some parents were so busy that they tried to beg off until their employer was called and told about the experiment. All of a sudden, they were willing to give it an honest try. They grew to love it and looked forward to visit at least once a month. The kids became more interested in school and tried harder when it became difficult. The average grades were higher at the end of the second year, and the children did much better on the mandatory tests for their grades.

Scheduling for the visit of the parents is somewhat complicated at first. When it starts working, all the problems become smaller, and the patterns are set. Most of the parents didn't want just two visits and wanted to visit the year around. That was very good.

It is a very bad thing when the parents bad-mouth the classroom and the teacher to their own children. We addressed this within the book and are hopeful the parents will realize they be positive or negative catalysts in the lives of their children and even the other children in the area. It is also hoped that the teachers will accept the parents and have something for them to do while they are in the classroom. The will see how their children act and react to various things. They will find the children will soon forget their parents are present and return to their normal day. Schedules will have to be made with the desires of the parents and where there are not too many parents in the classroom at one time.

If the parents are inadequate in their school skills, this would be a good opportunity for them to bone up and have a refresher on certain subjects. They can learn from the teacher or their own children at home. If education becomes important to the parents, it will become important for the child. Ideas that may be developed in the schools can be carried out in the home, and the home can become an extension of the school, and school and home will produce much better citizens.

I never implied it would be easy, but I know it would be a lot of fun, and when kids have a good time, they will learn more and understand better.

www.ingramcontent.com/pod-product-compliance
Lightning Source LLC
Chambersburg PA
CBHW020254290526
45784CB00003B/1249